James McCosh

The Prevailing Types of Philosophy

can they logically reach reality?

James McCosh

The Prevailing Types of Philosophy
can they logically reach reality?

ISBN/EAN: 9783337235741

Printed in Europe, USA, Canada, Australia, Japan

Cover: Foto ©Thomas Meinert / pixelio.de

More available books at **www.hansebooks.com**

THE PREVAILING TYPES OF PHILOSOPHY

CAN THEY LOGICALLY REACH REALITY?

BY

JAMES McCOSH, LL. D., Litt. D.
EX-PRESIDENT OF PRINCETON COLLEGE,

NEW YORK
CHARLES SCRIBNER'S SONS
1890

The Riverside Press, Cambridge, Mass., U. S. A.
Electrotyped and Printed by H. O. Houghton & Company.

PREFACE.

THIS little work is, to some extent, negative and undermining; it points out a chasm in modern philosophy. I would not give it to the public were it not that I have previously presented the positive and constructive side in my larger work on " First and Fundamental Truth." I wish the two works to go together, as constituting what I have been able to do for fundamental philosophy.

Agnosticism is upheld and propagated in the present day by several influential men, such as Mr. Herbert Spencer and Professor Huxley. It is in the air, and our young men have to breathe it and suffer the consequences. It is evidently exercising a relaxing influence on the faith and doctrinal convictions of the rising generation. It is in my view the grand office, at present, of the higher philosophy, to meet and expose this doubting spirit.

The question is, are the philosophies of the day fitted to do this?

With our eyes open, we are apt to look on the scene at some distance, rather than on things that are pressingly near and supposed to be known. So it is with modern metaphysicians (it was different with the ancient Greeks);[1] they direct their attention to more remote objects rather than those which are close to us, such as Reality.

We know self and certain things around us as Real; as having τὸ ὄν, Ens, Being, Existence. Now this Reality requires to be carefully considered by students of the First Philosophy, as Aristotle happily called it. I am to show that Reality is a truth to be assumed, and that no attempt need or should be made to establish it by mediate proof. Of those who have made the attempt, it will be found that they have more in the conclusion than they have in the premises, and that in fact they have assumed reality in order to prove it.

Mr. Spencer, the most comprehensive speculator of the day, has brought philosophy to a crisis. He is doing for later speculation, especially that of Kant and Hamilton, what Hume did for the systems of Descartes, Locke, and Berkeley, that is, bringing them to a *reductio ad absurdum* by showing that they deprive us of all knowledge of the nature of things. Philosophy has to start anew on the track of realism. I am not satisfied with the agnostic position of Spencer; I am also dissatisfied with the replies commonly made to him;[2] they have tried to prove reality, instead of showing that we are entitled to assume it.

I am aware that the realistic views presented in this work are so different from the prevailing ones — are, in

---

[1] See *Appendix A*.　　　　　　[2] See *infra*, p. 47.

fact, so revolutionary — that it will be needful to press them upon the attention of thinkers before they are adopted. This will have to be done by men who have greater influence among metaphysicians than I have been able to attain. Of the ultimate reception of these views on Reality (it may be somewhat modified) I have not a remaining doubt.

I acknowledge my obligations to my pupils, Professor Ormond of Princeton College, and Professor Armstrong of the Wesleyan University, Connecticut, for suggestions offered in the construction of this work; as also to another pupil, Professor Winans, Professor of Greek, Princeton, for aiding me in the collection of passages exhibiting Aristotle's doctrine of knowledge which I have stated in the Appendix.

CONTENTS.

SECTION I.

PAGE

WHAT IS REALITY? 1

SECTION II.

THE EXPERIENTIAL AND SENSATIONAL SCHOOLS 11

SECTION III.

THE A-PRIORI OR KANTIAN SCHOOL 18

SECTION IV.

THE SCOTTISH SCHOOL 37

SECTION V.

THE RESULTS REACHED 44

APPENDIX.

A. ARISTOTLE ON THE COGNITIVE POWERS OF THE MIND . . . 58

B. DOCTRINE OF DR. THOMAS AQUINAS 60

C. RECENT CRITICISMS OF KANT 63

D. PLACE OF INDUCTION IN METAPHYSICS 66

THE PREVAILING TYPES OF PHILOS-OPHY: DO THEY REACH REALITY LOGICALLY?

SECTION FIRST.

WHAT IS REALITY?

I.

EVERYBODY knows Reality; or, to vary the phrase when we speak of things acting, every one knows Actuality.

Of all thoughts, or perhaps I should rather say of all perceptions, it seems to be the clearest. Yet it is one of the most difficult to explain, or even express. This is simply because it is so simple: it does not admit of analysis; it has no distinct elements into which to resolve it, and there is no common genus or species under which to place it. The only way of showing its nature is to point to examples of it. We look on the wall of the room in which we sit, and know it to be real. We see a bird flying, and know it to be an actuality. We are conscious of ourselves in pain, and we are sure of our own existence in a state of pain.

There may be realities which we cannot discover: we do not know whether the planet Jupiter is inhabited. But there are things which we know to be real. We know body as it is presented to us as extended and exercising power or properties. In self-consciousness we know self as feeling, knowing, willing. Thus we know the manifestations of body, such as shape, resistance, and mobility. Thus we know the manifestations of self, as knowledge, desire, resolution. The qualities which we perceive in ourselves, specially such as love, benevolence, justice, are actualities. All these differ from imaginations, say a fairy, a ghost, a mermaid; and commonly the two can be distinguished. We call the one real, the other unreal.

II.

We cannot explain or even understand the facts of which we are conscious without calling in two cognitive powers, the external and the internal senses. These cannot be resolved into anything else, say, as is often attempted, into sensations, impressions, ideas; for none of these contain cognition, and cannot, therefore, give us knowledge by accumulation or combination. Nor can knowledge be drawn from them by reasoning; for, not being in the premises, they cannot reach it, except by falling into the acknowledged fallacy of having more in the conclusion than in the premises.

In acquiring a knowledge of external things, sensations are involved; feelings in the organism by all the senses: but these not having knowledge cannot give it to us logically. In looking at the table before us, there is the exercise of coats and humors, of rods and cones, and of the optic nerve; but we do not notice these in vision; their existence has been made known to us by the physiologist. In hearing, the tympanum, the hammer, the stirrup, and auditory nerve do not form part of our intuitive knowledge; they are merely the means of giving an exact field to our perceptions, but are no part of the real-

ity directly perceived by us. With these concurrences
we look immediately upon the thing, as we look through
perfectly transparent glass upon the tree without notic-
ing the medium.

In standing up for realism it is to be understood that
we hold by the known actuality of mind, with its perceptions, thoughts, and feelings, as well as of matter with
its extension and force. We have as clear a perception
of the one as of the other. We know both by a power
of intuition or direct inspection; the one by perception of the senses, the other by self-consciousness. We
know each of them by its peculiar properties: the one as
resisting our energy and extended in three dimensions;
the other, as knowing and judging with appetencies and
feelings. We possess these knowing powers naturally;
we carry them with us at all times; they are in our very
nature and constitution.

It is to be noticed that we know not only body and
mind: we know the affections or qualities of both; indeed,
it is by, or rather with, their qualities that we know the
substances. We know extension and solidity in matter;
cognition and emotion in mind. In particular we should
insist that we know moral qualities, such as good and
evil, and the obligation lying upon us to do the one and
avoid the other. It is of the utmost importance in ethics
to claim that there is a known reality in these moral
qualities, quite as much so as there is extension in body
and perception in mind.

III.

But it is asked contemptuously, Do you really believe
that we perceive things as they are? that things really
are what they appear to us? If you say so, then you
must hold that a man in a mist is larger than when in

clear air; that the sun when setting has a more expanded surface than at midday; that the sky is not an expanse, but a concave firmament; that the ocean as we look on it from the shore is a perfect level, without any curvature; that the lines in a railway draw nearer to each other as they recede; that a measured mile seen across an arm of the sea is longer than when seen across hill and dale on land. Such puzzles seem to show that, whatever supposed things be, they are not what they appear to us to be. Pointing to these difficulties, sceptical philosophers argue that we can never discover realities. The great body of philosophers employ themselves in showing how reality is to be reached by a process which they point out. I believe that none of the theories which they advance are satisfactory.

In order to remove the perplexities which have gathered round the subject, it is of importance to clear up two points: First, what are the realities which we profess to discover? These are:—

1. All that we know by intuition, that is, by an immediate perception of the object. Thus we know matter as extended and resisting our energy. We also know mind as knowing, thinking, feeling, resolving. Of this intuitive knowledge there are three criteria clear and decisive. First, it is self-evident. We know the object at once on looking at it. In looking at the table, I am sure there is a colored surface before me. Being thus self-evident, it is, Secondly, necessary; we cannot be made to believe otherwise. Thirdly, it is universal, that is, held by all men on the objects being presented to them. These are the tests of primary truths, and they sanction the conviction that we know realities. 2. All that is drawn from this by logical deduction. Ever since the time of Aristotle we have had a test of the legitimacy of inference

in the syllogism, which is expounded in the treatises of formal logic. 3. All that is got by scientific induction. We have tests of the legitimacy of this in the Prerogative Instances of Bacon, and more especially in John S. Mill's Canons of Induction, expounded in the books of Inductive Logic. To this class of realities belong the ascertained laws of nature, such as gravitation, chemical affinity, the association of ideas. In these we rise above the individual facts revealed by external and internal perception, and correlate the facts. The laws thus reached are not apodictic, or demonstrative like mathematical truths. But they are to be accepted provisionally as realities, which, it is allowed, may be modified and rectified by advancing discoveries; thus gravitation is a reality, but may possibly be resolved in the end, as its discoverer believed, into a higher reality.

IV.

Secondly, in order to determine the precise reality, we have to draw certain distinctions. I have unfolded these elsewhere,[1] but to make our discussion complete it is expedient to repeat them here, and apply them to the subject before us. Our object is to determine the reality, and we have: —

1. To distinguish between the real object and the sensations and feelings associated with it; generally between our sensations and perceptions. The former of these have indeed a sort of reality as affections of self, and they have no external reality, and we fall into error when we suppose that they have.

2. As the most important, we have to distinguish between our original and acquired perceptions. From an

---

[1] See *First and Fundamental Truths*, part ii. book i. ch. iii.

early period of our lives, during infancy and at all later dates, these two are closely associated with each other, and it is at times difficult to distinguish them. We claim a certainty in our original perceptions only; there may be error in our derived perceptions, and no reality in them.

I believe we can determine precisely what we know intuitively and directly by the various senses. The eye gives us a colored surface, nothing more. Hearing gives us a sound in the ear, from which we argue a cause, which is found by science to be undulations. In smell we have an affection of the nostrils; in taste, an affection of the palate; in touch proper, or feeling, an affection of the part from which the afferent nerve comes. In the muscular sense and energy, we have resistance offered, implying resisting energy. These are our primary sense-cognitions, all noticed by self-consciousness; they reveal realities, and upon them, by legitimate processes, we may rear other knowledges, also of reality, as derived from what is real. But we may also draw erroneous deductions when we pass beyond our intuitive knowledge. We do not know distance intuitively by the eye or by the ear, and we declare that the rock seen across the sea is only one mile distant, when actual measurement finds it to be two. I have shown that to preserve us from error we have to draw a like distinction in memory between our original memories and our constructed memories, in which latter there may be errors.

3. There is the distinction between the Primary and Secondary Qualities of Matter. This distinction has not always been correctly enunciated, but, when properly viewed, it has a most important place in determining what reality there is in the supposed qualities of matter. The Primary Qualities, such as extension and resisting

energy, are perceived, as Reid has remarked, directly; and are in all matter, as Locke has shown. These always imply realities. The Secondary Qualities are reached by argument, and the conclusion may not be correctly drawn. Thus in heat there is a reality in the organic sensation; but the external cause, supposed to be a mode of motion, is discoverable only by a scientific process, to be tested by the canons of induction.

By calling in such obvious principles and distinctions as these, we are able to stand up for the trustworthiness of the senses. What we see intuitively by the eye is not the sky, or the sea, or the rock, or the man in the mist, at a distance, but the object on the eye which is always real.

We are thus able without difficulty to determine what is real within us and around us more satisfactorily than is commonly done by metaphysicians, by a process which, if we examine it, will be seen to reach reality only by unknowingly assuming it.

V.

As to this knowledge, it should always be understood that it is only partial. "We know in part." This doctrine is opposed, on the one hand, to Gnosticism, which claims to know all; and, on the other hand, to Agnosticism, which professes to know nothing. Between these two we should hold by Mereognosticism, which holds that we know, but only in part. What we do know we should stand by, or rather stand upon, as a foundation to give us stability, and on which we may rear other realities.

As we all spontaneously believe in, or rather know, reality, so it should have a place, a deep and a thoroughly pervading place, in all philosophic systems. Whatever else philosophy may be, it is a science of foundations, and should commence with and rest upon the reality of things as a basis. An intellectual system which does not contain and embrace actuality must be a speculation rather than a philosophy.

We should not attempt to prove reality by mediate proof. Indeed, it cannot be demonstrated by any such process. The very constitutive principle of Logic or inference is, that there be nothing in the conclusion which was not contained in the premise (or premises). If reality be not in the premise, you cannot legitimately get it in the conclusion. The conclusion we reach here is, that in all philosophy we must assume reality. Beyond this we can do nothing more than show that we are entitled to assume it.

Not that it is to be represented as unproven and unprovable; it has its proof in itself. Not that it is to be described, as it often is in the present day, as unknown and unknowable; it is the first known, the best known of all truths. We need not try to prove it by mediate evidence, for we have immediate evidence, which is stronger, as on it mediate proof must depend in the last resort. It does not need other evidence, it has its evidence in itself; it is self-evident. It does not require external support; it stands on its own basis, and gives support to other truths. You cannot find any other truth clearer or more certain by which to establish it. Any external probation might rather unsettle it as tending to throw it off its proper foundation. We do not reach it by a process; it is rather the starting-point of many processes. It is not a conclusion reached; it is a premise necessary to innumerable conclusions.

It is possible, indeed, speculatively and in words, to

deny reality. But naturally and spontaneously we know all the while that the very denial implies the existence of one who makes the denial. A man may affirm that the river before him does not exist; but he shows that he believes in its existence by his declining to cast himself into it. He may say there is no carriage on the road before him; but he hastens to go out of its way when it approaches. He may insist that there is no sword in that man's hand; but he turns aside when it would pierce him. He may assure us that he does not exist; but in the very declaration he manifests his own existence.

Now, the question I have to ask is, What do the leading philosophic systems of the day make of reality? I am to put this question to each of them. Do they acknowledge it, or do they deny it? Do they accept it in whole, or only in part? Do they attempt to prove it, or simply assume it?

Some acknowledge that there is reality in certain objects and deny it in certain others, both of which are supported by the same intuitive evidence. Thus some claim that there is actuality revealed by the external senses, but not by the internal sense, and are landed in materialism. Others hold firmly by what we know of mind or self, but discard the fleeting phenomena of bodily senses, and are idealists. Some seriously try to prove the existence of reality; but as they evidently fail, there are others who feel as if we have only a phenomenal world, or a sort of dreamland. The fault of the great body of metaphysicians has been that they have acted on no principle, and have admitted actuality in some cases and denied it in others, both having a like evidence or want of evidence; and have thus made philosophy capricious and inconsistent.

Let us understand definitely what is the question I put. It is not what is the belief held and acted on by the system-builders as individuals, for practically they have all acted on the reality of things. David Hume said again and again, "Though I show what are the sceptical issues of the philosophy of the day, in actual life I believe and act as other people." Nor is my question how the philosophers wished their systems to be understood. Locke and Kant both held that their systems were realistic; but both philosophies, it can be shown, were idealistic on the one hand and sceptical on the other in their logical tendencies. We may be sure that all philosophies will issue sooner or later at the place to which logic drives them.

There is a Nemesis in philosophy as there is in morality. Hume the sceptic was the Avenger who drove to its consequences the errors that prevailed from Descartes to Berkeley. Herbert Spencer is the Avenger who is leading on to Agnosticism the error that has remained in the prevailing philosophies. We shall have to inquire how we are to build on the ground which has been left waste.

Philosophy in this age takes three types: I. The SEN-SATIONAL and EXPERIENTIAL; II. The A-PRIORI or KANTIAN; III. The SCOTTISH. These stand before us as mountain chains with valleys between, but with ranges of hills proceeding from them, and at times joining on to each other. They are found not only in Great Britain and America, but in Germany, France, Italy, and all civilized countries. The question I put is, What do these make of reality?

SECTION SECOND.

I.

THESE are not the same, though they are commonly connected.

The Experiential. Locke may be regarded as a representative of this school. He is not a sensationalist, though he is often so designated. Often have I heard him spoken of in the lectures of German professors by the name of Locké, as the representative sensationalist. But Locke allots to man two inlets of ideas, sensation and reflection; and attaches the greater importance to the second. To reflection we are indebted for all our ideas of mind and its qualities, of spiritual things and of God. Besides, he gives to mind a special power of intuition which perceives at once the agreement and disagreement of ideas (not of things), and thence rises to demonstration;[1] and he affirms that ethics might be made demonstrative, though he never showed how this could be done.[2]

Locke was personally a determined realist, and believed that his philosophy was realistic; but he never reached a full and satisfactory reality. Primarily, according to his theory, we perceive ideas within ourselves; knowledge is simply the perception of the agreement or disagreement of ideas, and we get all our ideas and know-

---

[1] *Essay*, b. iv. ch. i.   [2] *Essay*, b. iv. 17.

ledge by experience, which is limited, and can never rise above itself, any more than water can rise above its fountain. The consequence is, that he was never able to reach truth above experience, to universal and necessary truth holding true in all time and in all places. He believed most firmly in God and in infinity; but, as Hume showed, he could not by mere experience prove the existence of a God who is beyond all experience of sense and consciousness.

His greatest admirers were never able to show how he could find, on his theory of knowledge, an actuality external to the mind. He tells us: " 'T is evident the mind knows not things immediately, but only by the intervention of the ideas it has of them."[1] His whole account of human understanding proceeds on this principle. He fondly held that the ideas were resemblances and representatives of things; but he had no proof of this, and did not pretend to have any. The mind perceives ideas, but does not perceive things, and therefore cannot possibly know that the ideas which it knows are copies of the things which it can never know. We are thus shut up into an ideal world, and have no means of breaking out from this shell or prison, and can never know that there is such a thing as body beyond our idea of it.

Berkeley started from this position, and followed out Locke's theory to its legitimate consequences, maintaining that ideas are the reality, and constitute the whole of the reality which man can find. Hume interposed at this point, and drove the whole process to scepticism, — to what would now be called agnosticism. We have impressions, and ideas the reproduction of impressions, and have and can have nothing else.

[1] *Essay*, iv. 1.

II.

Sensationalism had already appeared in the philosophy of Thomas Hobbes, who derived all our ideas and knowledge from sensation, and allowed that we could never reach a spiritual reality in man or God. But what is specially called the sensational school originated with Condillac, who left out the Reflection of Locke, took no notice of his power of Intuition, and represented all our ideas, even the highest, as " transformed sensations."

In Great Britain the school has had a series of able men holding by Sensationalism, in James Mill, John Stuart Mill, G. H. Lewes, Alexander Bain, and in part Herbert Spencer. All of these have proceeded more or less fully on the negative and sceptical principles of David Hume.

We may take JOHN STUART MILL as the representative British sensationalist, as he sees more clearly than any other the logical consequences of the system, and is candid enough to admit and defend them. Body is defined by him as the " possibility of sensations," and mind as " a series of feelings aware of itself." [1] Almost every intelligent reader has felt this to be a very scanty remnant of the knowledge which we thought we had of ourselves, and of the persons and objects around us. Most people have felt it to be a *reductio ad absurdum* of the whole system. Naturally we think that we have more than this in body and mind ; that we perceive body as having extension and a power of resistance ; that we are conscious of mind as having intelligence and moral perception. But Mr. Mill is a clear and candid reasoner, and these are the legitimate results of the sensational system. You can get something higher, say personality

---

[1] *Exam. of Hamilton*, and my work, *Exam. of Mill.*

and intelligence and conscience only by introducing them from without, surreptitiously to clothe the nakedness of the system.

GEORGE HENRY LEWES holds the doctrine of Reasoned Realism.[1] He admits that "the ordinary man believes that the objects he sees, touches, and tastes do veritably exist, and exist as they are seen, touched, tasted." This doctrine is at once rejected. His system is Realism, "because it affirms the reality of what is given in feeling; and Reasoned Realism, because it justifies that affirmation through the ground and processes of philosophy, when philosophy explains the facts given in Feeling." Observe here that feeling is all in all. "The reality of an external existence, Not-self, is a fact of Feeling; Knowledge in all its manifold varieties is a classification of virtual feelings." His general conclusion is: "Mind is a form or function of Life." The Moral Sense consists of certain organized predispositions that spontaneously or docilely issue in the beneficent forms of action, which the experience of society has classed as right." Surely this is a very meagre account of the high qualities of which we are directly conscious in mind.

ALEXANDER BAIN says: "Mind possesses three attributes or capacities: (1) It has Feeling, in which I include what is conveniently called Sensation and Emotion. (2) It can act according to Feeling. (3) It can think." Consciousness is the same attribute of mind as "Feeling and Emotion." Thinking consists in discovering Difference and Agreement, and in Retentiveness; and it proceeds by the laws of Contiguity and Similarity. The Moral Faculty is resolved into "Prudence, Sympathy, and Emotions generally." In this list of man's

[1] *Problems of Life and Mind*, pp. 263, 287.

powers we miss those which raise him above this world and ally him to God. In regard to the independent existence of body his language is ambiguous. " There is no possible knowledge of the world except in reference to our minds. Knowledge means a state of mind." The latter clause is correct. The former may mean that we know matter simply as related to us, whereas we know it with qualities of extension and force, as having an existence independent of our existence. Mind and matter are not at all carefully distinguished; they are represented as the opposite sides of the same thing, as if the soul, which is spiritual, could have a side except in a metaphorical sense.[1]

In France, where Sensationalism so prevailed at the end of last century, it may suffice to look to II. TAINE, the present representative of the system. He makes Intelligence to consist largely of names, images, and ideas. He reduces ideas to a class of images, and images to a class of sensations. Names are a class of images. The laws of ideas bring back the laws of images. Mind is an aggregate (*polypier*) of images. In itself, external perception is a true hallucination. We have found that the objects that we call body are only internal phantoms; that is, the fragments of one detached from them in appearance and opposed to them, while in reality they themselves are the self under another aspect. So much for body, which he makes so illusory. As to moral personality, that which makes the continuity of a distinct person, it is the continued renaissance of the same group of distinct images.[2]

It may seem as if sensationalism is a very inoffensive,

---

[1] *Mental and Moral Science*, pp. 1, 8, 24, 250, 433 ; *Senses and Intellect*, p. 250.

[2] Taine, *De l'Intelligence.*

as it is a very simple, creed. But, if truly believed in, it arrests the growth of all higher aims and aspirations, moral and spiritual.

In closing this survey I may refer to TH. RIBOT, who has given us many valuable facts as to the relation of mind and body, but as a philosopher is a sensationalist, undermining in his journal that high school of philosophers who appeared in France in the second quarter of this century, including Cousin, Saisset, Simon, and others.

III.

In this criticism, I have been looking at the men solely in regard to their ability to find actuality. Locke was personally a believer in things without us, as we naturally apprehend them; but could get no proof of their existence, as he held that the mind can perceive only its own ideas. Of the sensationalists proper, some have no other reality than sensations or feelings modified and transformed, and have not reached and cannot reach things without or within us. None of them have a belief in man's personality and continued identity as evidenced in memory. None of them can rise to truth beyond experience, to truth necessary and universal. None of them acknowledge that we perceive immediately moral good, or that we can stand up for an immutable and eternal morality.

Meanwhile two formidable men have appeared to carry out the empirical doctrine to its logical results. Professor Huxley expounds and defends the doctrine of Hume slightly modified. He represents the mind as having Impressions, which he divides into — A, sensations; B, pleasure and pain; C, relations between these. This is a very meagre account of the furniture of the mind; yet this is all that is left.   There is not a thing knowing, nor a thing known.

At this point Herbert Spencer has come in.[1] He is so far a sensationalist. He identifies mind with the action of the nerves; but he does not, and cannot on his system, attribute to mind the perception of any moral or spiritual truth. He argues most resolutely for the existence of things ; but his argument is not conclusive, unless he assumes in his premises the reality which he professes to prove. He insists that, while we know that things exist, the nature of these things is unknown and unknowable. He believes in God, but it is the unknown God to whom the Apostle saw an altar dedicated as he entered Athens. I am glad the Avenger has appeared. He has shown conclusively that sensationalism shuts us up into the bottomless pit of Agnosticism. As people see this, they will draw back, and feel the necessity of assuming more than nerves, or sensations and feelings.

[1] *Study of Psychology,* pp. 48, 144.

SECTION THIRD.

THE A-PRIORI OR KANTIAN SCHOOL.

I.

LOCKE's Philosophy was the prevailing one from the date of his "Essay on Human Understanding," in 1690, to about 1830, when there was a shaking of thought, which issued in the second French Revolution and the Reform Bill of England, and a reaction in philosophy against the prevailing empiricism among conservative minds afraid of the too rapid advances of radical and revolutionary opinions. Since that time — indeed, fifty years prior in Germany — Kant's philosophy has been the prevailing one among deeper thinkers all over the thinking world. It was set up to oppose the scepticism of Hume, which awoke Kant, as he tells us, from his dogmatic slumbers. It was also meant, following Leibnitz, to counteract the empiricism and supposed sensationalism of the "very celebrated Locke," as Kant designates him.

It embraces a vast body of profound truth firmly concatenated, and has brought out more fully than was ever done before some of the deeper powers in the human mind. It reached the highest crest of the wave at the centenary, in 1881, of Kant's great work on the "Kritik of Pure Reason." I may be mistaken, but I think I see signs of late years of its being subjected to a severe ques-

tioning on the part of those who think that some of its
principles are keeping us away from reality. In one of
its forms, that of its high speculative ideas, it has gone
up years ago into the clouds of Hegelianism, from which
sober thinkers are turning away; in another form, in
which it has only appearances and unknown things, it
has run aground into the clay of the Agnosticism of Herbert Spencer, whom one half of our ambitious metaphysic
youths are following, and the other half are criticising.
It is time that we have a thorough criticism of the critical philosophy, such as we had half a century ago of the
philosophy of Locke.

For years past I have been urging general objections
to the system of the great German metaphysician.[1] In
this paper I am simply inquiring whether it has reached
and embraced reality.

The Kritic of Pure Reason, reared as a castellated
structure strong and compact, is the Ehrenbretstein of
German philosophy. It is a skilfully constructed, but is
an artificial and not a natural product. It will be seen
as we advance that it does not begin with reality, and so
cannot find it as it goes on, nor end with it logically. It
keeps reality at a distance, lest it should lead into materialism, which pretends to be so real. But Realism embraces both a material and a spiritual actuality, and each
should have its own place in a natural system in which
there is a body provided, where the spirit may dwell and
appear in living form.

II.

1. *The Method pursued, the Critical, does not reveal
Reality to us.* Kant acted rightly in departing from the

---

[1] See my work, *Realistic Philosophy*, vol. ii., article on " Criticism of Critical Philosophy."

Dogmatic Method, which had been used by Descartes and so many philosophers prior to his time. That method is used in mathematics, where we have axioms to start with, which we need only clearly to define. But it is not applicable in sciences which deal with scattered facts, and which we should pursue in the Inductive Method, in mental science, with self-consciousness as the agent which makes known the facts to us.

Kant takes credit for introducing a new Method, neither the Dogmatic nor the Inductive, but the Critical. Pure Reason, he says, can criticise itself. By this Method he constructed his system, which has been the admiration on the part of profound thinkers, even of those who may not regard it as the plan of Nature or of God. I acknowledge that criticism has a function to perform : it has to examine the works constructed by man, such as literary style, theories of poetry and the drama, works of art, as paintings, statues, and buildings. But we do not venture to criticise the works of Nature and of God ; our business is simply to discover what these are, and to fall in with them. No one has ever ventured to construct physical science by criticism ; say chemistry, or biology, or physiology. Were such an attempt made, it would issue in a series and succession of systems jostling each other, with no means of effecting a settlement. These effects have actually followed from the application of the critical methods to mental philosophy. Since the days of Kant, there has been a succession of systems superseding each other with no principle of final appeal. Every few years there appears a fresh and independent youth, proclaiming : Kant has not followed a certain principle to its consequences ; let us carry it out thoroughly. It was thus that philosophy advanced from Kant to Hegel. Another says, There is a grand principle which has been overlooked: let us introduce it and it will mediate between the systems; and thus a new system has been introduced to multiply the confusion. This was the mode of procedure in ancient physics, and the Stoics had one cosmology, and the Epicureans another. All this has been abandoned in modern science ; and we have a means of settling disputes, not by criticism, but by conformity of theories to the facts of Nature. The Critical Method has carried us away from Reality, and should now be let down from its high place as chief, to occupy a subordinate position.

There is a sense in which the truths both of physics and metaphysics are to be submitted to criticism. The profound wisdom of Bacon insisted on the inductive sciences beginning with " Necessary Rejections and Exclusions," and Whewell insists on the " Decomposition of Facts." But this is merely to put irrelevant matter out of the way to enable us to study by induction the facts of our nature without and within us.

Metaphysical philosophy is the science of First and Fundamental Truths, and these are to be discovered solely by the careful observation of what passes in our minds. But let it be understood that our induction of them does not give to these truths their validity ; it merely enables us to observe them. This is a distinction which I have been laboring to make students of mental philosophy see and acknowledge and proceed on.[1] Induction certainly does not give authority to Primitive or *A-Priori* truth; but it is necessary in order to our being able to discover its nature, and to use it in philosophy. The careful induction of Newton did not make, create, or invent the law of gravitation, or give to it its function ; but it was necessary to make it known to us.

[1] See *Appendix D.*

Such fundamental and necessary truths as personal identity, substance, causation, moral obligation, responsibility rising to a knowledge of God, are in our very nature,
and have their authority in themselves and from God.
But it is one of our highest prerogatives that we can rise
by internal reflection and induction to the precise knowledge of these truths, and use them in philosophy and
theology.

The Kritik of the Speculative Reason embraces three
points: I. ÆSTHETIC, or the *a-priori* elements in the
Senses; II. ANALYTIC, or the *a-priori* elements in the
Understanding; III. DIALECTIC, or the *a-priori* elements
in Reason. I am to subject these to an examination.

III.

2. In ÆSTHETIC *he misses Reality by making our
primitive perceptions look to phenomena and not to things.*
What is meant by phenomenon? In scientific investigation it is commonly used to denote a fact revealed in
order to be referred to a law. But in the philosophy of
Kant it is employed, in the original Greek sense of the
word, as an appearance. According to Kant and his
school, the mind in sense-perception and in self-consciousness begins with phenomena in the sense of appearances.
This, it can be shown, prevents it from reaching realities.

It might be argued that appearance of itself implies
reality; a phenomenon is a thing appearing. In one of
Longfellow's poems, there is a dispute between the tree
on the river's banks and the tree reflected in the waters
as to which is the reality. The question can be settled;
there is a reality in both, but of a different kind. The
tree on the banks has solidity, the tree in the stream is a
reflection of light. In all appearances presented to us,

there is a thing that appears, and what we have to ascertain is the precise actuality. It can be shown that this was the search of the Greek philosophy. In the Kantian system there is an appearance presented, but this appearance is entirely subjective; that is, in the mind. The mind in perception cannot look beyond itself, and so cannot know anything external. He argues, indeed, in the preface of the second edition of the Kritik: "The real existence of things outside of us, and independently of our consciousness of them, is an assumption without which he could not have found even a beginning for his philosophy." I am glad to find him making such an assumption ; it is an assumption given us by our consciousness. But he tries to prove it by a very doubtful probation. " The simple but empirically determined consciousness of my own existence proves the existence of objects in space outside of me." I cannot see that the conclusion follows from the premise. Whether assumed or proven, it is clear that he holds by the existence of external things; but the nature of these external things cannot be known by us. Even the mind itself is not known as a thing. This is one of Kant's most pernicious errors, more so than even his denial that we know anything of the nature of matter. Nothing remains, as we shall see forthwith, but a conglomerate of forms, categories, and ideas, embracing no reality beyond themselves.

We now see where Herbert Spencer and the Agnostics of our day get their views and their nomenclature. They deny that they are sceptics, and that they do not believe in a reality of things; but then they affirm that the nature of things cannot be known by us. Mr. Spencer thinks that there is a God, but then he is unknown and must ever be unknowable by man.

Kant draws the distinction between phenomenon and

noumenon, — between the thing appearing and the *Ding
an Sich*, the thing in itself, or, as Dr. Mahaffy translates
it, *the thing per se*. The distinction will come before us
once and again. It is an altogether unsatisfactory one.
We cannot know that a thing exists without knowing
something about it, without knowing it under the aspect
in which it makes its existence known to us.[1] In sense-
perception we know not only that the thing before us,
say that book, exists, but we know it in part; we know
it as a colored surface. We are certainly not omniscient;
we do not know all about any one thing, about ourselves,
or other things. But we know what we know, know so
much of the thing, not, it may be, of the thing in itself,
which is meaningless, as a thing cannot be in itself, but
of the thing, the very thing. In denying this, which he
does, Kant is undermining realism, and leaving us in the
darkness of nihilism.

IV.

3. In ÆSTHETIC and ANALYTIC he *makes us perceive
things, not as they are, but as made or modified by forms
in the mind.*

First, our perceptions or intuitions by the senses and
by self-consciousness come to us under the forms of
Space and Time, — Space being the form of the bodily
senses, and Time being the form both of the external and
internal senses. We are not to look on these two forms,
Space and Time, as having any objective existence, any
independent or real being. They are forms in the mind
imposed on what we perceive. It follows that we do
not and cannot know the world without us, nor even the
internal self as it is. We perceive everything as through

---

[1] I have all along been insisting on this. It is confirmed by Zeller. See *Appendix C.*

stained, and it may be twisted glass, which gives its color and form to what comes under our notice. At this point Kant's idealism enters, and it runs on through the whole of his philosophy, till, as we shall see, it culminates in pure idealism. In opposition, Realism holds that Space and Time, as well as the things contained in them, are realities, and are what we intuitively perceive them. We know matter—so much of matter; we know mind—so much of mind; and we also know space and time, in which matter and mind are—so much of space and time. As having such a knowledge, we believe in the mathematical truths derived from them by legitimate inference. If we allow, with Kant, that they are not objective realities, we shall be constrained by logic to hold that the things perceived, body and mind, are also ideal. We notice a *body* in *space* and an *event* in *time*, and we have the same evidence, an immediate evidence, of the existence of all four, the body, the space, the event, and time.

Secondly, the mind begins with the perceptions of sense, and then the understanding pronounces judgments upon these. The judgments are pronounced according to mental forms called Categories. Great pains are taken to show how these Categories are deduced. They are very much the same as the judgments of the Aristotelian or Formal Logic, of which Kant was professor:—

I. QUANTITY:
   Unity,
   Plurality,
   Totality.

II. QUALITY:
   Reality,
   Negation,
   Limitation.

III. RELATION:
Inherence and Subsistence,
Causality and Dependence,
Reciprocity of Agent and
   Patient.

IV. MODALITY:
Possibility and Impossibility,
Existence and Non-Existence,
Necessity and Contingence.

I am not concerned to examine these forms, or determine whether they are the best possible classification of judgments. Modern logic makes the judgments fewer. But they have been made greatly more scientifically correct by the criticism of Kant. Here, however, our inquiry is simply, Have we come nearer to actuality? On the contrary, we have gone farther away from it. We have subjected what we know of it to a farther modifying process. These Categories, which are all merely subjective, impose themselves upon the concepts which have been formed by space and time being imposed on the sensibility. The place allotted to the Real seems to me to be very artificial and awkward. He does not place it in Æsthetics, or the domain of the senses; we do not immediately perceive it. He places it in Analytic, under judgment. The Real which he reaches is a mere form in the mind, not implying anything objective out of the mind. Taking this view, the tendency of the German philosophy has been ever towards idealism. Even the sensationalists among them, in reducing all our powers to sensation, do not regard our sensations as giving us a knowledge of things.

One of the Categories is Cause and Effect. It obliges us to look on every event as having a cause, but this does not prove that it really has a cause; we can be assured of this only by the experience of sense, which cannot rise above what we experience, and cannot therefore give us any universal truth. We would prove that a God exists . arguing from the world, which is a visible effect, — "a manufactured article," as Sir John Herschel expresses it, — to a cause in God. But the argument is invalid, as we are not allowed to assert that causation is universal. As Hume argues, we are not entitled, from causation in our limited experience, to infer a causation in world-making, which is beyond our experience. The same may be said of all the twelve Categories, as unity, as existence, as necessity; they carry no weight beyond the experience of sense. It thus appears that ÆSTHETIC, or the science of the senses, does not give us things as they are; that ANALYTIC, or the science of the understanding, takes us farther away from things; and we have now to turn to DIALECTIC, which inquires what reality there is in these processes of sense and understanding.

V.

In the Æsthetic and Analytic, Kant is building up: starting with phenomena formulated by Space and Time, and going on to the Categories, or the various forms of logical judgment. Under the head of Dialectics, he inquires what validity there is in the structure which he has reared.

Rising above Sense, rising above Understanding, the mind can form Ideas of Pure Reason, as he calls them. These are Substance, the Interdependence of Phenomena, and God. These Ideas give us a Rational Psychology, a Rational Cosmology, and God. We feel now as if a domain were thrown open to us wide and pure as heaven itself. We hasten to enter it, and hope that we have here a lasting possession where we can abide forever, and hold communion with the loftiest thoughts. But Kant proceeds to tell us that this grand scene is a mirage.

Kant is too powerful a logician not to see, and too honest a man not to admit, that these Forms of Sense and Categories of the Understanding cannot give us known and objective existence. He uses stronger language than I have done in expounding his system, in showing that neither sense nor understanding can reveal reality. They do not profess to give it to us: they cannot give it, for they do not themselves have it. Hitherto he has been rearing an edifice, stone upon stone, all of Cyclopean dimensions. Now the giant takes as much pains to pull it down. The constructive work is ended; the destructive work begins. As Hamilton puts it, the intellectual Samson pulls down the house upon himself.

As to Substance, we have an Idea of it, and it seems to stablish us; but it is only a form in the mind. He examines Descartes' fundamental argument, " *Cogito ergo sum.*" If the *ego* be in the *cogito,* it is all a mere assumption; if it is not in the *cogito,* we cannot put it in the conclusion without having more in the conclusion than in the premises.

As to the Interdependence of Phenomena, he labors to prove that, on the supposition that phenomena are facts and not mere forms, we are landed in a succession of contradictions or Antinomies. As an example, we are led, on the one hand, to hold that the world has a beginning in time, and, on the other, that it has had no beginning in time. For myself, I hold that pure Reason alone cannot establish either of these positions; but Kant holds that it can prove both, and that the two counteract each other and leave us only zero.

As to the Idea of God, we are obliged to contemplate Him theoretically, but we can prove his existence only on the principle of cause and effect; but we have no evidence that this is universal, and so the argument is not conclusive. Speculatively there is a God, logically and really there is no proof of the existence of God.

Let us realize the position to which we have been brought. Let us see where we stand, on rock or quagmire. In Sense we have some reality in phenomena which are subjective, but imply an external reality. In Understanding we have less reality, but we have subjective Categories binding the appearances. In Reason we have only the ghosts of departed realities. Our inheritance does not consist of coins, but only of paper currency with no guarantee behind.

It might seem as if in being led to do all this work, and passing through all these difficult passages, we had been deprived of our promised wages. But Kant denies this, and reminds us that he has never given us any assurance of our finding reality. There is no deception, for there has been no promise. But he admits fully and proclaims decidedly that there is *Illusion*. We all fall naturally and necessarily into the illusion, just as when we stand on the shore we see the ocean level and not rounded ; just as when we look up into the sky we see it as a vault and not an expanse.

VI.

Kant calls in Moral Reason to save us from the nescience of the speculative Reason. This Moral Reason announces a fundamental law : it is expressed in the Categorical Imperative (an admirable phrase), and is simply a modification of our Lord's supreme law, " Do unto others as ye would that they should do unto you." It is, " Act according to a rule which might be applied to all intelligences." This implies that man is free, and as a corollary that he is responsible ; that there is a judgment day, and therefore a future life, and a God to guarantee the whole. Morality, immortality, and God are thus bound up together.

I think that Kant means us to understand that he has here reached reality. The moral law and its corollaries, freedom, responsibility, and a judgment day, are all actual existences. He thus held resolutely by great truths which preserve us from scepticism, and lead the way to and guarantee other truths. I am inclined to think that he meant these moral truths to sanction the validity of the truths of the speculative reason, specially the existence of responsible beings who are under the moral law. He thus counteracts by his moral principles the nescience of his speculative principles. Viewed under this aspect, the tendency of his philosophy is all for good.

However, it has been doubted whether he can reach and retain an independent moral reason in consistency with his speculative nescience. The nescient principle carried out logically, seems to bear against the moral reason quite as much as the speculative reason. How does moral perception come in? He says that the senses alone have the power of intuition which he denies to the Reason. But if the reason have no power of intuition, how can we come to discern and appreciate moral good? If it comes in by the gate of sense, shaped by the Categories and idealized by pure reason, then we are landed in nescience by the moral reason as we are by the speculative reason. Whatever may be Kant's doctrine on this subject, it is evident that his moral law, if it has any meaning, must apply to living beings who are supposed to be under it; but we can know that there are such beings only through the forms of sense, the Categories of the understanding, and the ideas of pure reason; and these he shows are illusions. I do not see how he can logically reach the reality of the moral power, or the corollary which he derives from it, the existence of God. From ideal, that is, illusory premises, we can draw only ideal and illusory conclusions. From ideal facts we can infer only an ideal God: this in truth seems to be all that some of the theologies of Germany have.

It has been urged all along — ever since the publication of the "Kritik" — that Kant is inconsistent in standing up for the reality of the moral, and denying that of the speculative reason. I believe that both stand on the same foundation, which is a foundation of reality. But, whether consistently or inconsistently, Kant has done immeasurable good by standing up so resolutely for the reality and validity of the Moral Reason.

VII.

I may notice here the tendency for the last few ages to acknowledge that the intelligence of man leads to infidelity, from which we may be saved by Faith or Feeling. This style of speaking was derived from Kant and Jacobi, and has been adopted by many German, British, and American thinkers. They tell us, with a sigh, often of affectation, that the understanding leads to scepticism, and then, with Jacobi, call in faith to lift them out of the slough. I do not believe that there is any such schism in the mind which God has made in his own image. I deny that one part of our nature contradicts another. I deny that the understanding, following its laws, issues logically in scepticism. I am sure that he who thinks that intelligence ends in scepticism will not be brought back to truth by a loose appeal to faith. The sceptic who has attacked the validity of reason, having tasted blood, will, on a like principle, attack the trustworthiness of faith. I am sure that intelligence and faith both reveal truth to us, each in its own way; the one of things that are seen, the other of things that are not seen.

In the philosophy of Kant there are two powerful but discordant elements, the ideal and the nescient, each of which has produced its proper effect. The ideal ran its course in the first instance; passing through Fichte and Schelling, and culminating in Hegel, being pantheistic throughout. I do not wonder that Kant, who wished to be regarded as a realist, was offended with Fichte, who seized certain of his principles and followed them out to a pure idealism. Schelling worked to correct the one-sidedness of Fichte, and brought in object as well as subject; but made the two identical and both subjective, so that he can have no objective reality. And what shall I say of Hegel? He has dived down into depths and mounted into heights to which I cannot follow him, and in which human logic, as it appears to me, has no place. When I find that he employs his *a-priori* powers to set aside the demonstration of Newton, that he holds Being and Not-Being as identical, that Being and Thinking are the same, and that contradictories may both be true, I regard his system as a *reductio ad absurdum* of the whole of his philosophy. I have heard in Berlin an eminent professor of his school proving to his own satisfaction that all is one: that you and I, God and Nature, mind and body, truth and error, good and evil, are all one. In his all-comprehensive system, which embraces everything, he has a reality claimed by him, but it is a reality merely in his *a-priori* forms. He would turn away with disdain from the reality which I am pleading for, and which insists that we intuitively know things as they are.

VIII.

Upward of two hundred works have been published in Germany, besides dozens in other countries, on the philosophy of Kant, who has been almost deified for one hundred years by his followers, as Aristotle was deified for five hundred years in mediæval times. Most of the works are liable to the objections which I have taken to Kant. There are some, however, who are longing for reality in philosophy, and, perceiving that Kant has not furnished it, have endeavored to discover it by a course of their own. But they have been so bound as by cords with the forms of Kant, that they have not been able to break forth into full and independent liberty.

In seeking to avoid the extremes to which Hegel led his admirers, there has been a loud cry of "Back to Kant!" I believe this to be a wiser course than to go on with Hegel or beyond him. Kant's Kritik is, after all, a more consistent structure than that of any of his followers. In many of his logical analyses, and in his ethical principles, he has expounded truths on which the mind may rest in the assurance that it will never be moved. But should philosophy be brought back to the position of Kant, being in a state of unstable equilibrium, it will run on in one or other of the courses which Kantism has hitherto followed, either with idealism or agnosticism; or, more probably, with an incongruous mixture of the two which will not amalgamate.

In examining the New Kantian School I have fallen in with a work by Stähjen, which seems to me to state and review the more eminent systems of that school fairly and searchingly, and I take advantage of the criticism urged.[1]

There is Lange, author of a learned and elaborate work, "History of Materialism." This is esteemed by the New Kantians as the most philosophic performance

[1] *Kant, Lotze, and Ritschel*, by Leonhard Stähjen, translated by D. W. Simon, Ph. D.

of the present day. The author is regarded as an apostle
of the Kantian view of the world, and the leader of the
new movement. Says Stählen: "It is decidedly and at
once significant of the direction which Lange's thought
takes, that he sets aside the realistic factor which Kant's
theory of knowledge endeavored to retain." "The thing
in itself is simply a limitative or regulative conception.
We do not know whether things in themselves exist."
"His own presuppositions leave him no alternative but
to teach that the entire phenomenal world, as well as the
organs by means of which it is apprehended, are a product of our representation."

There is Lotze, whose instructions have been attended
by so many English and Americans as well as Germans.
He has a kind of reality. He assumed "the existence of
an infinite multiplicity of simple beings which constitute
the basis of the world of sense, and, after Herbart's example, designates them the Reals. In Lotze's view, these
same Reals are of the nature of souls, spirits, because of
their independent existence." Surely all this is a speculative fancy, which explains nothing, and of the existence
of which we have no proof from sense or consciousness.
"What, then, becomes of the world of sense? It is a
mere phenomenon; and not even objective phenomenon,
but phenomenal in a purely subjective sense." Space
and Time are ideal. "But if space is a mere form of
subjective intuition, that which we intuite in space is as
exclusively in us as space itself; outside of us there is
nothing. Time also, in like manner, is a form of intuition; the temporal-spatial world itself is phenomenal."
He proceeds a step farther. "According to Lotze, the
being of things is a standing in relations. It is of the
very idea and essence of that which exists to stand in
relations; there is no such thing as existence without

relations; there is no other sort of actual existence but the standing in relations."

Stählen seems to be justified in his strong statements. "The corner-stone of the Kritik of Reason is, we do not know even ourselves as we are in ourselves, but merely as we appear to ourselves." He concludes: "The edifice of the Kantian philosophy has fallen in ruins before our eyes, crushed beneath the weight of its own contradictions; and even the ruins themselves have disappeared in a bottomless pit. In so far, therefore, the result of the critical system is null. We have seen that it cannot possibly be the system of truth; that, on the contrary, the consequences are utter illusion and nihilism."

While Kant had a strong ideal element, he had an equally strong — in the end a stronger — nescient element. It is affirmed that the mind begins with phenomena in the sense of appearances, and can never know things as they are, either without or within us; in fact, either body or mind. This view, as we shall see immediately, was adopted so far by Hamilton, and from him has been taken up by a powerful speculator who has the advantage of a large acquaintance — as an amateur — with physical science, who argues powerfully that things exist, but with equal power that we can never know their nature. We see now how it is that Agnosticism is so prevalent; is, in fact, the prevalent heresy of our day. Professor Huxley, President of the Royal Society of London, who sits in the chair of Newton and has adopted the scepticism of Hume, and Mr. Spencer, who is so influential a thinker, have brought us to this blank issue. Agnosticism is in the air, and our young men are obliged to breathe it as they read the pages of many of our popular journals. Not that the writers or readers are able to follow the concatenated reasoning of Kant,

Hamilton, and Spencer; but they catch the results, and carry them out to their practical consequences.

But our souls cannot live in this void any more than our bodies can live in a vacuum, and there must soon be a rush out of this confined, this dark and damp malarial cellar, into the free and open, the pure and healthy air, where we can live and breathe, walk and run.

SECTION FOURTH.

THE SCOTTISH SCHOOL.

I.

THIS school has not so much influence now as it had at the end of the last century and the beginning of this, when it was the only philosophy taught in Scotland, and had large power in France where it met the prevailing sensational philosophy, and when it was expounded in most of the colleges of the United States. In Scotland it has able and independent supporters, though Kant and Hegel divide the dominion with it. In France and the United States it has a traditional influence for good, where its sound and safe principles are taught by many professors, who are unaware of the source from which they have drawn them.

The founder of the school was Francis Hutcheson, who, in general philosophy, held with Locke that all that is perceived by the mind are ideas; but Shaftesbury brought in a number of other senses besides the sensation and reflection of Locke, such as the moral sense and the sense of honor. The true representative of the school is Thomas Reid, a careful observer, a sincere lover of truth, an independent thinker, carefully avoiding all rash speculations. He had two great ends in view in all his writings. The one was, to lay down principles in opposition to his contemporary, David Hume, who was undermining all natural and moral truth; the other end was, to overthrow and set aside Locke's theory of ideas, which seemed to him to come between the mind and things, and thus to be the main support of the scepticism of Hume.

II.

To accomplish the first of these ends, he called in Common Sense. The phrase and the doctrine are defended by the erudition of Sir W. Hamilton; but they are somewhat ambiguous. Besides its Aristotelian meaning, where it denotes the percepts common to all the senses, it has two meanings in conversation and in literature: it may signify good sense or sound judgment in the affairs of life — said to be the most uncommon of all the senses — or, the principles of thought and belief common to all men. It is only in this latter sense that it can be used in philosophy. Less ambiguous phrases may be employed to denote this last quality, say "fundamental laws of thought and belief," employed by Reid's disciple, Dugald Stewart. Thus expressed, it may be maintained that the doctrine of Reid and his school met Hume more satisfactorily than Kant did with his greater logical power.

To accomplish his second point, Reid gives what he regards as the true account of sense-perception. He argues most conclusively that we cannot arrive at a knowledge of the external world by reasoning. He unfolds what he regards as the mental process in sense-perception. There is first a sensation produced by the external object; then there is a perception suggested instinctively by the sensation. The *instinctive suggestion* seems to me to be as little satisfactory as the idea of Locke. He does not give the mind, with Aristotle, a knowing or gnostic power. It is thus by an indirect or mediate process that we reach reality. It does not appear that the mind can directly perceive ; that is, know the thing.

He further holds that we do not perceive things, but only the qualities of things, which imply the existence of things. This doctrine is not announced so openly by Reid, but is emphatically declared by Dugald Stewart. Neither has expressed the true doctrine, which is, that we perceive things, the very things, by sense-perception. We perceive things by their qualities.

III.

Sir William Hamilton is the most erudite of the Scottish metaphysicians. In this respect he is worthy of being put alongside of the great German scholars. He gives us quotations, with critical strictures, from obscure writers of various ages and countries. In all his discussions he uses a sharp, two-edged sword. He was brought up in the school of Reid, and boldly defended him when the younger metaphysicians were beginning to assail him because of his caution. In his lectures on Logic and Metaphysics, afterward published, he travels far beyond the narrow field cultivated by the Scottish School. He has made very valuable contributions, and thrown out very definite opinions in regard to all the mental sciences, except, perhaps, Ethics, which he does not seem to have specially studied.

IV.

The Scottish School generally, especially Dugald Stewart, give a high place to moral perceptions. In this respect they are all realists, except Thomas Brown, who makes virtue consist in mere feelings. None of them allows that the mind is capable of rising to a positive idea of infinity. Hamilton argues powerfully, with British philosophers generally, that our idea of infinity is merely negative, though he seems to allow that, while we have no positive idea of infinity, we have a faith in it, — as if we could believe in a thing of which we have no idea. Surely there must be some way of showing that, as we think and talk intelligently about infinity, eternity, omniscience, we must have some positive though necessarily inadequate idea of it. I maintain that we have an idea of something that is beyond our widest concept, and is such that nothing can be added to it.

We have here to do simply with the relation of Hamilton's philosophy to Realism. He professes throughout to be a realist. Those things we immediately perceive are the real things. " The material reality is the object immediately known in perception." " The very things which we perceive by our senses do really exist."[1] But he studied the philosophy of Kant, with which very few Scotchmen were at that time acquainted, and, perceiving the common points of agreement between the Scotch and German schools, he sought to combine them. But they will not coalesce. Hamilton reached and expounded a doctrine which seems to me to conflict with the realism of Reid. He adopted and defended with great logical ability the doctrine of Relativity. " Our knowledge is relative, first, because existence is not cognizable absolutely and in itself, but only in special modes ; second, because these modes thus relative to our faculties are presented to and known by the mind, only under modification, determined by these faculties themselves."[2] My readers will notice that here we have thoroughly Kantian principles, which cannot be grafted on the realist stock. In the three general propositions, and in the sev-

[1] *Met.*, vol. i. pp. 279, 289.   [2] *Met.*, vol. i. p. 148.

eral clauses, there are an immense number and variety of assertions wrapped up. Some are commonly entertained, but others are joined on to them, from which I strongly dissent. I acknowledge, first, as self-evident, that things are known only as we have the capacity to know them; and this is limited. I acknowledge, secondly, that we do not know all things; nay, that we do not know all about any one thing. In other words, that our knowledge is partial or finite, as distinguished from perfect or absolute. I may admit, thirdly, that man discovers internal objects only under a relation to himself and his cognitive powers. So much I allow. But, on the other hand, I demur, first, to the Kantian statement, that we do not know existence in itself, or, as he expresses it elsewhere, that we do not know the thing in itself (*Ding an Sich*). I do not like this language: it is ambiguous; when thoroughly sifted it is meaningless. I doubt much whether there can be such a thing as "existence in itself," and of course what does not exist cannot be known. If he means that we do not know things as existing, I deny the statement. Everything we know we know as existing; not only so, but we know the thing itself; not all about the thing, but so much of the very thing. Then I demur, secondly, to the statement which is thoroughly Kantian, that the mind in cognition adds elements of its own. As Hamilton expresses it: "Suppose that the total object of consciousness = 12; and that the external reality contributes 6, the material sense 3, and the mind 3. This may enable you to form some rude conjecture of the nature of the object of perception."[1] To suppose that in perception or cognition the mind adds anything, is a doctrine fraught with destructive consequences; for, if it adds one thing, why not two

[1] *Met.,* vol. ii. p. 129.

things, or ten things, or all things, till we are left in absolute idealism, which means absolute nihilism?

Hamilton is logical enough and candid enough to admit the issue. Comparing his philosophy with that of Germany, he says: "Extremes meet. In one respect both coincide, for both agree that the knowledge of nothing is the principle or consummation of all true philosophy, — *Scire nihil; studium quo nos laetamer utrique.*" But the one doctrine, openly maintaining that nothing must yield everything, is a philosophic omniscience; whereas the other, holding that nothing can yield nothing, is a philosophic nescience. In other words, the doctrine of the unconditioned is a philosophy confessing relative ignorance, but professing absolute knowledge; while the doctrine of the conditioned (Hamilton's doctrine) is a philosophy professing relative knowledge, but confessing absolute ignorance."[1] I confess I always feel chilled when I read this passage.

Hamilton's learned follower in Oxford, Dr. Mansel, in his famous Bampton Lectures, used his principles to undermine Rationalism in religion; but in so doing he undermined, without meaning it, religion itself, as he did not leave to us those great truths of Nature which conduct us to revealed religion.

V.

At this place Spencer comes in. It is evident that he was much swayed by and started from the position of Hamilton and Mansel, whose philosophy was the reigning one in Great Britain at that time. Many think, and I agree with them, that he followed out their doctrine to its logical conclusion. I do not see that Hamilton's prin-

---

[1] *Discussions*, p. 609.

ciples can stop short of the Agnosticism of which Spencer is the ablest expounder. I pressed Dr. Mansel to meet the downward current; but he never did so, and Hamilton's pupils have not done so. Thus Hamilton and Mansel are charged with opening a flood-gate through which destructive waters are flowing, producing issues which they never contemplated.

Sir James Mackintosh and Dr. Chalmers, who were trained in the Scottish School, were greatly delighted when, in their later life, they discovered the close resemblance of the German and Scottish philosophies. The two agree in standing up for what the one called *a-priori* and the other fundamental principles. But while they agree they also differ. The main difference is, that, in discovering what these principles are, the one proceeds in the Critical and the other in the Inductive Method. The one discards observation; the other uses it, not indeed as the foundation of first truths, but the means of discovering them. I am trying to give the proper place to the induction which is so recommended by Reid, Stewart, and Chalmers, and which is fitted to keep philosophy from the extravagances into which it is so apt to fall, and which can be corrected only by its being ever compelled to fall back on facts and the observation of facts.[1] Just as logic is an expression of the processes of the mind in discussive thought, so is Metaphysics the expression of what passes in the mind in discerning primary truth. The exact expression is reached in both cases by a careful observation of the mind in the respective operations.

[1] See *Appendix D.*

SECTION FIFTH.

I.

At the close we may take a look backward at the ground over which we have traveled.

Experiential Philosophy cannot give us universal or necessary truth, or any truth beyond the narrow limits of observation. It is doubtful whether it can furnish a valid argument for the existence of God. In the system of Locke we are supposed to perceive only ideas, and are precluded from the knowledge of things.

Sensationalism gives us sensations and feelings variously compounded, and we cannot from these derive mind or even body as substances, but only, as Mill concludes, "possibilities of sensation" and "a series of feelings aware of itself."

The a-priori School of Kant makes our first perceptions to be of phenomena (appearances) and not of things. Then all that we know has *Forms* imposed upon it by the subjective mind, so that, while we must believe in the existence of things, we do not know what they are. We pronounce judgments upon them, but according to the restrictive laws of subjective *Categories*. The result is, that, when we would argue the existence of substance, cause, and other connections, and of God, we find ourselves in a world of *Illusions*. A vigorous attempt is made to save us from nescience by calling in Moral Reason, which gives us a high idea of duty, of a judgment day, and of God, which are all real; but it is doubtful whether the system can legitimately give us a known world of things to which to apply them. It is evident that an ideal world can give us only an ideal or pantheistic God.

THE SCOTTISH SCHOOL proposes to be, means to be, and professes to be realist; but in the pages of Reid and Stewart it speaks doubtfully about our perceiving things, and in the pages of Hamilton it gives us only relative knowledge, which is not a knowledge of things as they are, and ends avowedly in nescience.

II.

I have shown that Hamilton was led into agnosticism by the critical philosophy of Kant; and Mansel applied this doctrine to overthrow rationalism. It was when Hamilton and Mansel were in the ascendant that Herbert Spencer began to think and write on these subjects, and drove the prevailing doctrine to agnosticism. He argues powerfully that we are constrained to believe that things exist; but he maintains as resolutely that we do not and cannot know the nature of things. It can be shown, as I have done in various parts of my works, that we cannot know that things exist except we know so much of their nature.[1] Without this, any predication of their nature would be meaningless; it would be a predication about something unknown, and we could have no apprehension of what the predication referred to. This is the position to which Kant and Hamilton have brought us, and it is now occupied by Mr. Spencer: that things exist, but that we do not and cannot know their

[1] See *Appendix C.*

nature. Spencer shows that, while we have sensations, which are simply affections of the nerves, and can pronounce judgments upon them, we have, and can have, no insight into what they are.

III.

If there be any truth, even partial truth, in this representation, philosophy has come to a crisis, such as it did when Berkeley drove the partial idealism of Descartes and Locke to pure idealism, and Hume drove the whole school to nihilism. Speculations have thus been shown to be false by the consequences to which they lead. The vessel has foundered because it has not followed the right track. The train has been wrecked by the bursting of the materials which it carries. As philosophy has inflicted the wound, it must hasten to heal it. It must begin to build anew (for the human head, not to speak of the human heart, will not be satisfied with an agnostic philosophy) ; and it will have this advantage, that the ground has been so far cleared of incumbrances. I trust it will rise as a phœnix from its ashes, profiting by the blunders it has made, and purified by the fires through which it has passed.

Realism is the one thing to be introduced into modern philosophy (it will be shown that it had a place, though not always the right place, in the ancient Greek philosophy) to give it coherence and consistency. Philosophy, whatever else it may do, aims at settling foundations. But reality is the firmest of all foundations. A chink has appeared in the wall, indicating that there is some insecurity at the base. There are crevices staring us in the face, and they have to be filled up. We may find that these evils can be remedied by giving reality its proper place in the rock on which the building stands, and in the cement which binds the parts together. In this process some abutments which are incumbrances will require to be taken down; but the edifice will rest more firmly upon its well-laid foundation.

We see how it is that Agnosticism is so prevalent in the present day. Young men, pondering a deep subject in religion, in morals, or science, with which they are troubled, find that philosophy, with all its professions and pretensions, gives them little to rest on in the last resort; and they conclude that nothing can be known as it is. Those who would confute this Agnosticism experience great difficulty in doing so. The reason is, that they have no ground, no ποῦ στῶ, on which to stand. They commonly satisfy themselves with proving, which they can do easily and successfully, that nescience is suicidal. It is an evident contradiction to affirm that we know that we can know nothing. But they do not see that in establishing this point they are only playing into the hands of the agnostics. For by far the most powerful argument of Hume and the sceptics is, that there are contradictions, antinomies (as they call them), in our nature, and so conclude that human reason cannot be trusted. They set two strong contradictory propositions before us that counteract and arrest each other, and leave nothing between. Many an ambitious youth is laboring to pull down Mr. Spencer's imposing structure only to find it falling on himself. He propounds an argument which seems profound; but, on searching it, it is seen to assume the reality which he proposed to prove. The only successful method of meeting Agnosticism is to assume reality; not trying to prove it, but taking it for granted, as we do the axioms of geometry as an intuitive truth, which can stand the tests of intuition.

IV.

It is acknowledged on all hands that we cannot prove every truth by syllogism, or by any mediate or external evidence. We can prove only by premises given and allowed. But, if we are to prove every truth, we have also to prove the premises, which have to be proven by prior premises; and thus we need an endless chain of premises hanging on each other, and the whole hanging on nothing. There are truths which do not require to be proven; they have their evidence in themselves, and we have an intuitive power of discerning it. Of this character are the axioms of geometry. No one should attempt to prove them; if any one does, he will find that the evidence he employs is not so clear and certain as the axiom itself is. We assume the axiom without seeking proof, and in doing so we are not acting unreasonably; we are assuming what we know by a higher reason than mediate reasoning. Spontaneously we are sure that we have reality in what is presented to us by the senses and by self-consciousness. I believe that this is the first truth which the infant mind knows as it wakes into existence. Being so, philosophy should take it up and start with it; it should not attempt to demonstrate it. If any one is not satisfied with this statement let him try to prove his own existence. What external proof can he bring? Perhaps he may answer, Some one, my father, told me so. But does he not see that, in order to reach the existence of the father, he has to assume his own existence?

V.

I am insisting that to every philosophy the question be put, What do you make of reality? If you omit it, I

demand that you give it a place; otherwise your system
is a mere speculation. If you give it a place, I ask, At
what place? — at the entrance? in the middle? or at the
close? In this inquiry it will turn out that reality cannot be proven except by premises that contain reality,
and that it is to be assumed in philosophy, even as it is
taken for granted and acted upon in our native perceptions.

Here it may be interesting to notice that the aim of
the Greek philosophy — the earliest deserving the name,
all prior being loose and undiscriminating — was to discover reality as opposed to appearances. Its earliest
metaphysical school was the Eleatic, and its search was
for existence, — τὸ ὄν and τὸ εἶναι. In their subtle disqui-
sitions, they often confused what is simple, and made
assertions which have no meaning. It can be shown
that the Greek philosophy kept it steadily in view to discover, not the absolute, as the German historians so
often represent them as doing, but the real. This was
the aim of Socrates when he insisted so much on defini-
tion. Plato found the real among the fleeting in his
Ideas. Aristotle classified the real under his ten Categories. The Stoics found reality specially in virtue as
the only good, and the Epicureans in pleasure. It was
because this was their search that the Greek philosophy
has been so abiding, and that students ever turn back to
it, while other systems have been swallowing each other
and have had only a temporary sway. So, then, as we
assume spontaneously the existence of a self and a non-
self, let us also assume it in philosophy, as the reflex
expression of our spontaneities. Philosophy should commence with it, and take it with it by implication wherever it goes. In all its investigations, it should presup-

pose and proceed upon it.   A philosophy without it is a speculation and not truth.[1]

VI.

The relation between mind and body has always been regarded as a mystery which we cannot thoroughly clear up. Yet we may reverently inquire what the process is, and state what it is so far as we know it. Mr. J. S. Mill has shown that all physical causation is dual or plural; it consists of two or more agents constituting the cause, and producing a change on each of the agents. A blow is inflicted on a man's brain which causes his death; here the cause is the blow and the state of the brain, and the effect, the death, is the joint result of the two. So in Sense-Perception there is an outward object, — it may be in the body or beyond the body, and thus standing in a particular relation to the mind ; the effect is the perception of the object. So, in all cases, there is a mutual affection of the external object, which in the last resort is the nerves and brain on the one hand, and on the other hand the mind, with its perceptive power; and the result is a perception of the object. This seems to be a statement of the facts. There is no doubt mystery, that is, some things which we do not understand ; but there is no more mystery than in any other causation: the two agents have the property of acting on each other. But if this be the true account, possibly after all only a partial account, we are delivered from all the useless intermediaries which metaphysicians of late ages have introduced to explain what they do not explain, and which may need no explanation. Aristotle briefly expresses the exact facts : "The sensible objects call the perceptive sense into activity."[2]

[1] See *Appendix A.*   [2] See *Appendix A.*

I am aware that in pursuing this course perplexities and difficulties will arise, as they do in all branches of investigation, physical and metaphysical; but there will be far greater difficulties in following any other course; for the reality which we have unnaturally shut out will ever be coming back to assert its existence, authority, and claims, and to disturb and confound the errors which have taken its place. It will turn out that, whatever mysteries may cast up in carrying out this assumption, there will be no positive contradictions; and the reality will hold its place when the spectres and illusions have been obliged to vanish in the light of actuality.

Of all things, it is most essential that we should know what is the precise reality which we intuitively know. This must be carefully separated, by the "necessary rejections and exclusions," from all adventitious circumstances, such as sensations and feelings.

We look through a perfectly transparent glass on a tree before us. What is it that we see? It is not the glass, but the tree; so when we take away the glass it is not the eye but the tree that we perceive. A like remark may be made of all the senses. Let us try to ascertain the precise object perceived by each of the windows of the soul.

In Sight what I perceive is not the retina and brain affection, but a colored surface. In the Muscular Sense I do not observe the nerve which moves the muscle in locomotive action, nor the nerve which carries up the notice of the motion to the brain; I perceive merely the muscle resisted by an object.

In Touch Proper, or Feeling, we do not discern the nerve, but merely the sensitive feeling which we localize at the point which the nerve reaches.

In Hearing I am conscious, not of the tympanum, the

hammer and stirrup, and other apparatus, but simply of a sound in the ear.

In Taste we know our palate as affected. In Smell we know our nostrils as affected.

By the last four of these we know directly only what are called Secondary Qualities of body; that is, special affections of body for which we are prompted to seek a cause beyond our organic frame, as it is not in our frame, and are commonly able to find it. By a combination of the perceptions of the primary and secondary qualities thus reached, we are able to form a knowledge of body, say of an orange : by sight, as extended, or in space and as colored; by the muscular sense, as having resisting force; by hearing, as capable of issuing sound; by touch, taste, and smell, as capable of rousing sensations of special sorts.

VII.

Having now an internal and external world, all of realities, we can add to them indefinitely by reasoning, and by the continued observations of sense and consciousness. Thus we can know not only the shape of this triangle, but by necessary inference that its angles are equal to two right angles. We have the moral law: " Do unto others as ye would that they should do unto you ; " but further, as a consequence that we should show kindness to this poor man, this negro, this enemy of ours, this slave, this criminal, and this infidel. We have the facts brought back by memory, the records of history, the discoveries of science. By these processes, conducted by ourselves and others whom we trust, we can increase our knowledge wide as the knowable world, and all be of realities.

But it is asked in a disdainful manner, Do you pre-

sumptuously propose to set aside all previous philosophies : that of Plato and Aristotle, of Descartes and
Locke, of Kant and Reid ? I answer at once and deci-
sively, I reject none of the great truths which have been
established by the great thinkers of the world, greatly to
the benefit of the world. I mean simply to settle some
of them upon a surer foundation. Some of them seem to
me to be resting on perishable piles, like the houses in
Venice ; I would found them on the rock of reality. In
some of them there are visible cracks and excrescences,
sceptical and ideal; I would fill them up by bringing in
the reality, which they have overlooked because it is so
near, and put it in the room of the incumbrances. We
may thus retain, and in a secure position, all that is true
and good in the systems of ancient Greece and modern
Europe.

VIII.

I acknowledge and claim, if the philosophy of reality is
assumed, amendments will require to be made on certain
of the prevailing philosophies, in the way both of addi-
tion and subtraction. Empiricists will have to take in
much that they have overlooked and omitted. Along
with their sensations and feelings, images and symbols,
they will have to accept and embrace higher truths, such
as self-personality, substance, moral obligation, which
are all realities revealed by consciousness. We have as
strong and quite as convincing proof of the latter of
these principles as we have of the former. The Scottish
School must be made to throw away its crutches of impressions, instincts, suggestions, and common sense, and
give the mind a power of seeing things directly. The
a-priori philosophy must be made to begin with things
material and mental, instead of subjective laws. It must

be led to regard space and time as realities quite as much as the objects we perceive in them. The Categories of the understanding must take the shape of, and be represented as, laws of the mind; such as cause and effect, which we perceive to be in the very nature of things acting. The higher ideas, such as substance, the connection of things and Deity, must be so apprehended and stated as to show that they are realities which we can know and believe in, and feel them to be the most steadfast and exalting truths which the mind can dwell on.

But it will be objected that in this realistic philosophy we seem to have no room left for idealism. I answer, that I leave to it its own province, which is one of the richest and most fertile which God has allotted to man; it is the region of imagination, with fancy and feeling to endear them to us. But we must keep idealism in its own province. We do not allow it a place in science, say in astronomy or chemistry, in social or political science. We do not permit it to attempt to improve or beautify the laws of gravitation, of animal and plant life, of the economic law of supply and demand. We insist on all these keeping rigidly to facts. We then allow idealism to come in and embellish them as it can. And the wider the sciences of fact extend their discoveries, the more extensive is the field opened to the play of the imagination. Now, there should be like restrictions and extensions in metaphysics as physics. We must settle what are first and fundamental truths by scientific investigation; and then, above this solid ground, we may allow a covering to be spread, rich as the clouds of the summer sky.

IX.

Agnosticism appears in a variety of forms. In particular, it takes a vulgar and a philosophic form. In the former, it is obliged to admit the sensible, but turns away from all the higher truths of God and immortality; of these, it is said, we can know nothing. It is obliged, in spite of itself, practically to acknowledge reality in the common affairs of life — at least in regard to meat and money; but would leave all spiritual truth in the regions of doubt and darkness. In this shape it is an impression and a vague credulity, rather than a fixed conviction and faith; and in arguing with it we feel as if we were fighting with a ghost. It is only when attacked that it takes the form of a fixed creed. Thus put it claims to a philosophy; and puts itself in the form of a general doctrine. It is of vast moment in these circumstances to have a decision in the final court of appeal, and to show that agnosticism is utterly untenable, being contrary to our fundamental cognitions. This is what I have endeavored to do in this treatise, leaving the vulgar agnosticism without a foundation.

X.

In closing this paper, I may remark that our spontaneous belief that we are in the midst of reality, gives us a feeling of assurance and stability in all the affairs, including the practical affairs, of life. It goes with us, and should be encouraged to go with us, wherever we go. It is the business of philosophy not to undermine and restrain it, but to explain and defend it.

Physicists, in their deeper researches, are ever coming to mysteries which they are apt to designate as metaphysics. What should they do in these circumstances? When there is a reasonable hope of going farther, they should just continue their researches on the method prescribed by the logic of science. But when they have come to a truly metaphysical truth, — when they have come to a first truth, to what is self-evident and necessary, to what shines in its own light, and rests on its own foundation, — then they should feel that they have come to the rock, and should rest and be satisfied. This they should always do when they come to what is self-evidently real. It should be one main end of metaphysical philosophy to furnish to them the tests of such truths, with an arrangement and classified list of them. This I have endeavored to do in my work on " First and Fundamental Truth." What is found deficient in that work will doubtless be supplied by others.

It is only on the supposition of things within and without us being real, that we have logical proof of the existence of God. " The invisible things of God are clearly seen, being understood from the things that are made, even his eternal power and Godhead." It is from *the things that are made* we get a legitimate argument for what we do not see, the existence of the Maker. As long as we look on what we perceive as mere phenomena, sensations, or subjective ideas, the God we reach must be of a like character, ideal or pantheistic.

Every student of the history of religion knows that philosophy and theology are apt to affect each other. A high theology has often elevated philosophy by bringing in its high ideas, so allied to religion and to God. A pretentious philosophy, passing beyond its proper sphere, has often corrupted religion. Even the grand systems of Plato and Aristotle have been made to corrupt the simplicity of the faith, as we may see in Origen, in the ancient Church, and in the scholastic writers of mediæval times, and in the pantheistic systems. The holy doctrines of the Church in Germany have had more influence than any other external power in constraining philosophy to look to the highest attributes of man, his freedom, his personality, and his immortality. A meagre theology, overlooking the higher perfections of God, has favored an empirical philosophy. The sensational philosophy has produced a theology which takes no account of the holiness of God. The rationalism of England, in the end of last century and the beginning of this, allied itself with the theory which accounted for all our ideas by association, and with utilitarianism. The ideal philosophy gives us an ideal theology, which tends toward pantheism, and has produced those plausible theories which have come over to us from Germany.

We claim to be formed in the image of God, and a realistic philosophy, teaching us to look to the various powers of man, should raise our faith to the contemplation of a full-orbed Deity: our understanding leading us to look on him as omniscient, our moral nature to regard him as holy and just, and our feelings to cleave to him as benevolent. The full truth revealed by theology and philosophy is: God is a Spirit; God is Light; God is Love.

APPENDIX.

APPENDIX A.

ARISTOTLE ON THE COGNITIVE POWER OF THE MIND.

EVER since Descartes, the Father of Modern Philosophy, drew so decidedly the distinction between mind and body, there has been a change of view among metaphysicians generally as to what the mind starts with in its intelligent acts, and as to the nature of sense-perception. Descartes, who was so resolute a defender of spiritualism, maintained that mind cannot act directly on body, nor body upon mind. To explain their evident intercourse, Malebranche, following Descartes, taught the doctrine of Occasional Causes; Locke called in Ideas; and Leibnitz advocated Preëstablished Harmony, to show how mind could know body. None of these theories could accomplish the end they were meant to serve; could in any way explicate the nature of perception by the senses. The Idea, as has been shown by Reid and Hamilton, only brought in new difficulties, only introduced officious intermeddlers. It may be profitable in these circumstances to turn to the views of Aristotle. These were commonly adopted by the schoolmen throughout the thousand years of mediæval times.

It is evident that he gives a higher, or rather a deeper, place to native cognition than is now done. In treating of the intellectual powers, the moderns speak of the Senses and of the discursive faculties of Judgment and of Reasoning, which is made up of correlated judgments. But they neglect to announce that the senses, external and internal, give knowledge of realities; and judgments imply real or imaginary objects, on which they are pronounced. Our judgments are always predications about something apprehended. They are the declaration of a relation between two or more things which, in the order of things and of time, must be prior to the judgments upon them. To judge or reason, we must have objects about which to judge or reason. The unit of thought is not, as Hamilton and most modern metaphysicians maintain, judgment, but cognition by sense-perception and self-consciousness. What we start with in intelligence is knowledge, and thus and then the judgment has materials on which to act, and may rise to higher cognitions of realities by observing further relations between things, and drawing conclusions.

The judgments may be about objects, imaginary as well as real. But imaginations are formed of things which we have experienced, put in new forms and dispositions. Our judgments about them do not make them real, but they imply a reality, from which the imaginations have been drawn. Our idea of a mermaid is derived from the woman and the fish. Our systems of Psychology will ever be perplexed and confused till they give knowledge of concrete things a primary place in the operations of the mind, and make judgment depend upon it.

Aristotle's Divisions of the Powers of the Soul. — I do not claim that the Stagyrite has stated all that I have now laid down, but he has given a higher or rather a deeper place to cognition than the moderns.

His penetration allured him to draw innumerable distinctions among the powers of the soul. It might be argued, I think, that all these proceed on real differences. But I have not been able to discover that he sums them up in a comprehensive unity. He does not profess to give an exhaustive and logical classification of the mental powers. The parts are not exclusive and independent.

Perhaps his most fundamental division of the faculties is that noticed by Sir W. Hamilton into the Gnostic and Orective, adopted by Aristotle's commentator, Philoponus.

This is a distinction, noticed not only by Philoponus, but by others who follow Aristotle, such as Thomas Aquinas, who, in philosophy, seems to me to be the most judicious of the schoolmen. (See Appendix B.)

In *De Anima*, II. 2, Nutritive, Sense-Perception, Discursive, Motive, θρεπτικόν, αἰσθητικόν, διανοητικόν, κίνησις.

Again, *De Anima*, II. 3, Nutrition, Sense-Perception, Appetence, Local Motive, Discursive Power, θρεπτικόν, αἰσθητικόν, ὀρεκτικόν, κινητικὸν κατὰ τόπον, διανοητικόν.

Again, *De Anima*, III. 10, Nutrition, Sense-Perception, Cognition, Will, Appetence, θρεπτικόν, αἰσθητικόν, νοητικόν, βουλευτικόν, ὀρεκτικόν.

Throwing out nutrition, which is a physiological process, and taking sense-perception and the discursive power together, as cognitive powers, and similarly together Will and Appetence, we have the two forms, the Cognitive and Motive.

He sums up the powers in two groups, under a different nomenclature : —

De Anima, III. 9, τὸ κριτικόν and τὸ κινεῖν τὴν κατὰ τόπον κίνησιν (τὸ κινητικόν) ; discerning and motive.

De Anima, III. 9, If a tripartite division of the soul is made, in each there is ὄρεξις, for Will is in the rational or intelligent part ; and in the non-rational part, desire and impulse, ἡ ἐπιθυμία καὶ ὁ θυμός.

So we have the Soul defined as that in which we live, perceive, and think, that is, the Vital principle, Sense-Perception, and Discursive Power, II. 2.

" The part of the Soul which is rational is divisible into two : the Will (βουλευτικόν), and the Intelligent (ἐπιστημονικόν). That these are different from one another, may appear from their objects (ὑποκείμενα). For as color and flavor and sound and odor are different from one another, so nature has made the perception of them different : sound we have through the hearing sense, flavor by the taste, and color by the sight; so, likewise, we must assume the same arrangement elsewhere, namely, that, since the objects differ, there are different parts of the soul by which we get knowledge of them. That which is perceived by the reason (τὸ νοητόν) is different from that which is perceived by the senses; and as we know both by the mind, there must therefore be a part which has to do with the objects of sense-perception, different from that which has to do with the things perceived by the reason." This last quotation is from the "Magna Moralia" (I. 35), which, if not written by Aristotle, was written by some one who felt his influence.

Aristotle on Sense-Perception. — There is the frequently quoted passage : "Sense-Perception is the power of perceiving the form (εἶδος) of sensible objects without the accompanying matter (ὕλη), just as the wax takes the figure of the seal without the iron or gold which makes the ring." *De Anima*, II. 12.

He enunciates what I regard as the true doctrine, and which I have quoted in the text. *De Sensu*, 2, τὸ αἰσθητὸν ἐνεργεῖν ποιεῖ τὴν αἴσθησιν.

He gives to the senses the power of a certain kind of knowledge. "Animals participate in a certain kind of knowledge, some more, some less, some, indeed, very little; they have sense-perception, and sense-perception is a certain kind of knowledge" : γνώσεώς τινος πάντα μετέχουσι, τὰ μὲν πλείονος, τὰ δ' ἐλάττονος, τὰ δὲ πάμπαν μικρᾶς· αἴσθησιν γὰρ ἔχουσιν, ἡ δ' αἴσθησις γνῶσίς τις. This passage is very decisive as to man, and all animals having knowledge, — a certain kind of knowledge. *De Anim. Gen.*, I. 23.

He assures us that the perceptions of the senses are always true, αἱ μὲν αἰσθήσεις ἀληθεῖς αἰεί. *De Anima*, III. 3.

He shows that the deceptions of the senses are merely apparent. He saw that the difficulties might be cleared up by attending to what each sense testifies, and separating the associated imagination and opinions, or judgments. *De Anima*, III. 1, 3, 6.

He tells us : "It is not possible to have knowledge till one comes to individual things." *Metaph.*, I. 2, 11.

He announces a realistic doctrine : "A man can think (νοῆσαι) whenever he wishes, but not so exercise perception, for the object must be there :" διανοῆσαι μὲν ἐπ' αὐτῷ, ὁπόταν βούληται, αἰσθάνεσθαι δ' οὐκ ἐπ' αὐτῷ · ἀναγκαῖον γὰρ ὑπάρχειν τὸ αἰσθητόν. *De Anima*, II. 5.

"The sensible object removed removes the perception, but the perceptive faculty, on the other hand (removed), does not remove the object of perception ": τὸ μὲν αἰσθητὸν ἀναιρεθὲν συναναιρεῖ τὴν αἴσθησιν, ἡ δ' αἴσθησις τὸ αἰσθητὸν οὐ συναιρεῖ. *Categor.*, 5.

Aristotle has not only individual senses, he has a master sense, τὸ κύριον αἰσθητήριον, or a common sense, κοινὴ αἴσθησις. This faculty distinguishes between the different sorts of Sense-Perception, sight, taste, etc., and synthesizes and comprehends various perceptions as belonging to one object, *De Anima*, III. " There is a common power which accompanies all the separate parts, by which the mind perceives alike that it sees and that it hears; for not by the sense of sight does the mind see that it sees; and it distinguishes, and is able to distinguish, for example, that ' sweet' is different from ' bright,' neither by taste nor by sight, nor by both these together, but by some common faculty (' mental part,' μόριον), working with all the instruments of sense-perception. For perception is single, and the master sense is single." *De Somno*, II.

It is to be regretted, I think, that at the time of Aristotle, and for some ages after, the Greeks had not given a place to self-consciousness. To it should have been allotted the power which the mind has of seeing that it sees. I believe it was not till towards the time of M. Aurelius, in the middle of the second century after Christ, that self-consciousness, συνείδησις, had a separate and important place allotted to it.

Metaphysicians will find it necessary in these times, when philosophical inquiry seems to be tending towards nescience, to look to and consider the views held by the great leader of thought for a millennium, and by those who were led by him. Reality, with the capacity of knowing it, is the one thing necessary to make knowledge consistent in itself, and consistent with our nature. It is the one thing needful to introduce in order to meet the agnosticism to which Huxley and Spencer are reducing all philosophical inquiry. The common opponents of Spencer and of agnosticism leave this out, and their replies are inconclusive, and are felt to be unsatisfactory.

APPENDIX B.

It may serve a good purpose to give the views of Saint Thomas, the angelical doctor, on the same subjects (" Summa Theologica," P. 1, *Quaest.* lxxxv. 6). He quotes Augustine : Omnis qui fallitur, id in quo fallitur, non intelligit. Aristotle is quoted as " the Philosopher " : intellectus semper est verus. He discusses his subject, and his conclusion is : Cum quidditas rei sit proprium objectum intellectus, nunquam contingit circa ipsum falli nisi per accidens, prout ipsi compositio vel divisio, seu discursus admiscetur, in quibus fallitur quandoque. He approves Aristotle : Sensus enim circa proprium objectum non decipitur, sicut visus circa colorem, nisi forte per accidens in impedimento circa organum contingente. He sums up : Ad *primum* ergo dicendum quod falsitas dicitur esse in mente secundum compositionem et divisionem. Et similiter dicendum est ad *secundum* de opinione et ratiocinatione. Et ad *tertium* de errore peccantium qui consistit in applicatione ad appetibile. Sed in absoluta consideratione quidditatis rei et eorum quae per eam cognoscuntur, intellectus nunquam decipitur.

APPENDIX C.

RECENT CRITICISMS OF KANT.

There are some indications that the recoil against the combined Idealism and Nescience of Kant has commenced. Dr. Hutchison Stirling announces emphatically that Kant has not answered Hume, and that never has the world been so befooled by a system as it has been befooled by the system of Kant. He uses very strong language. He declares the system of Kant to be " a vast and prodigious failure," and his method as only " a laborious, baseless, inapplicable superfetation." — *Princeton Review*, Jan., 1879.

I may quote a little more fully from Stählen : " Kant's aim was to vindicate the objectivity of human knowledge in opposition to the scepticism of Hume. This he deemed possible only

in one way, namely, by showing that that which gives objective
validity and necessity to our knowledge of things is to be found,
not in the things themselves, but in the human mind itself."
He goes on : " Kant's intention was to establish the reality of
our knowledge in opposition to the scepticism of Hume. But
what he meant to be a rescue turns out to be rather an entire
overthrow of the knowledge of objective truth. For the method
which he follows tends to show that what we know is merely the
phenomenal appearance, not the truth nor the thing itself." But
what is the phenomenal ? The answer is, " Phenomenon in the
Kantian sense *is not objective but subjective* phenomenon, that
is, it is not a coming to light or coming forward of the thing
itself, but purely a mode in which we represent things, an affection of our sensibility, a modification of our consciousness which
reveals nothing whatever of the nature of the thing as it is in
itself."

This, I may remark, is the very objection which I have been
taking for years past, that Kant makes the mind start with appearances instead of things, and that we cannot know things
except under forms imposed by our own minds. He insists :
" Objective knowledge, a knowledge of anything that has actuality outside and independently of our consciousness, there is
none." This is true not only of things external to ourselves,
but of the mind itself, as Kant is constantly asserting that " we
do not know even ourselves, but merely as we appear to ourselves." He says I have no right to say that a thing is, if I am
in entire ignorance how or what it is (p. 26), an objection which,
I may add, I have been constantly taking. I have been par-
ticularly pleased with the following extract from Zeller : —
" But, however unworthy of acknowledgment the prudence
with which Kant refrained from drawing the extreme conclusions of his idealism, it must not be forgotten that this very
course involved him in great difficulties. Not only when the
general postulates of his system were denied, but also when
these were admitted, there were still to be found many pro-
foundly critical questions left unanswered, many a doubt un-
solved. This was true especially of Kant's positions concerning

the thing in itself (*Ding an Sich*). On the one hand, for instance, on the supposition that direct experience presents things to us only under the forms of perception and thought, only as phenomena, the question could still be raised whether it had really been proven that the essence of things is of necessity unknowable for us, whether we possess no means of determining their essence through the observation and comparison of phenomena. If, on the other hand, the complete incognizability of the thing in itself was granted, the question still emerged, whence, then, can we obtain any knowledge of its bare existence? If I know absolutely nothing of *what* an object is, I cannot know *whether* it is, and *that* it is; for every assertion concerning the existence of a thing presupposes some concept of the thing whose existence is affirmed, no matter how incomplete this concept may be. When Kant endeavored to show the existence of things outside us, he understood by these at best some reality apart from us, which occasions our sensations; when he demanded belief in a Deity, he understood by Deity the independent cause of the world. When, on the other hand, he maintained that we can know absolutely nothing of the thing in itself, that it is an unknown *X*, a mere problematic or limitative concept, this required that he should leave it completely undetermined whether any reality apart from us exists at all. His explanation of the idea of cause as a category of the understanding, which as such is applicable to phenomena alone, should have prevented him from applying it to the thing in itself, from postulating this thing as the cause of our presentations. Nay, he should have gone further, and have said straight out that we have no ground for the assumption of the thing in itself, that it is of no service in the explanation of phenomena, that it only marks the limit of our activity, and as such it can in itself lie just as well within as without us. This deduction was in reality drawn before long in the Kantian school, the more readily, the more undeniable it is that Kant's refutation of idealism, and his moral argument for the existence of God, are far removed from the validity of strict demonstration." — Zeller's "Geschichte der deutschen Philosophie seit Leibnitz," pp. 414, 415 (second edition).

APPENDIX D.

THE OFFICE OF INDUCTION IN FUNDAMENTAL PHILOSOPHY.

I have had great difficulty in getting a hearing for one point in my philosophic views. In the discovery of *a priori* truth I allot an important function to inductive observation. This seems to identify me with the empiricists, from whom I entirely separate myself. I hold that there is no induction in the spontaneous exercise of intuition; it sees the object at once. But if we, as metaphysicians, express the law in a general form or law, we need to proceed by a careful observation, the facts being given us by self-consciousness. We have to inquire what is the precise *a priori* law, say of causation, as it manifests itself. If we neglect to do this, there is a great risk of presenting the principle in a mutilated, which is, so far, an erroneous form. The vagaries of metaphysicians commonly spring from an imperfect induction. But in calling in induction we do not give it an authoritative or guaranteeing office. Induction merely lets us know what the law in the mind is; it does not give it its imperativeness. It needs anxious inspection to find what the law of causation is, but the law operates whether we observe it or not. This distinction is easily understood by those disposed to give their attention. It saves me from the inconsistency and the imbecility with which I have been charged in a recent criticism. It gives to reason and to observation each its proper place in the construction of fundamental philosophy. It may be made the means of reconciling the Scottish and German philosophies.

FIRST AND FUNDAMENTAL TRUTHS. Being
a Treatise on Metaphysics. 12mo, $2.00.

Every thinking mind has occasion at times to refer to first principles. In this work the author sets himself earnestly to inquire what these are ; to determine their nature, and to classify and arrange them into a science.

" I value it for its large acquaintance with English Philosophy, which has not led him to neglect the great German works. I admire the moderation and clearness as well as comprehension of the author's views. While containing a large respect for the Masters of the Scottish Philosophy, such as Sir Wm. Hamilton, this has not restrained his independent judgment or kept him stationary."—*Dr. Dorner, in Jahrbuecher der Deutschen Theologie.*

" No philosopher before Dr. McCosh has brought out the stages by which an original and individual intuition passes first into an articulate but still individual judgment and then into a universal maxim or principle ; and no one has so clearly or completely classified and enumerated our intuitive conclusions or exhibited in detail their relation to the various sciences which repose upon them as their foundation. The amount of summarized information which it contains is very great ; and it is the only work on the very important subject with which it deals. Never was such a work so much needed as in the present day. It is the only scientific work adapted to counteract the school of Mill, Bain, and Herbert Spencer, which is so steadily prevailing among the students of the present generation."—*London Quarterly Review.*

THE EMOTIONS. 12mo, $2.00.

This work avoids the confusion arising from treating all mental states as feelings. It gives an analysis, description, and classification of them as distinguished from other mental qualities. There is a full treatment of the elements involved in the Emotions.

" Neither the Scottish philosophers nor any other philosopher who after them has treated the Emotions has so completely examined them as the author of this work.

" Speaking of his view of the beautiful, Literature and Philosophy can equally profit by this part of a work which we can point out as the most complete and broad ever written on the subject."—*La Filosofia delle Scuoli Italienne.*

" It is a duty and a pleasure for us to signalize in particular an instructive chapter on the association of the Emotions and Speech. Excellent description, fine analysis, and incontestable talent for exposition, equal to those of his predecessors in psychology."—*M. Ribot's Revue Philosophique.*

THE RELIGIOUS ASPECT OF EVOLUTION.
Second Edition. New. 12mo, $1.00.

CONTENTS : Chapter I.—The State of the Question. II.—The Organic History. III.—Powers Modifying Evolution. IV.—Beneficence in the Method of Evolution. V.—Final Cause in Evolution. VI.—Geology and Science. VII.—The Age of Man.

" The book is small, and the statements and inferences are condensed, but it is one of the best epitomes of the relation of the Creator to his earth in the process of creation that has been written."—*Hartford Courant.*

" He avows himself in favor of evolution, properly limited and explained, and in that opinion he will find himself in sympathy with a large and rapidly increasing class of educated, intelligent men."—*New York Sun.*

REALISTIC PHILOSOPHY. Defended in a Philosophic Series. 2 vols. 12mo. Vol. I.—Expository. Vol. II.—Historical and Critical. Each, $1.50.

The first volume discusses the great philosophic problems of the day, such as Energy, Efficient and Final Cause, Certitude and Prayer. The second treats of Locke, Hume, Berkely, Reid, Kant, Huxley, and Herbert Spencer.

"No thinker of our time commands a more ready or more general hearing. Conviction, clearness, and earnestness are apparent in his advocacy of the future philosophy of this country."—*Bishop Hurst.*

"Eminently cogent and instructive volumes designed for exposition and defense of fundamental truths. The distinct but correlated subjects are treated with equal simplicity and power, and cover in brief much of the ground occupied by larger publications, together with much on independent lines of thought that lie outside their plan."—*Harper's Magazine.*

GOSPEL SERMONS. 12mo, $1.50.

"The sermons are Gospel to the core. Something of poetic feeling occasionally voices itself, but the imagery is always for illustration and enforcement of the great truth under discussion."—*Sunday School Times.*

THE DEFENSE OF FUNDAMENTAL TRUTH.
Being an examination of J. S. Mills' Philosophy. 8vo, $2.00.

"The spirit of these discussions is admirable. Fearless and courteous, Dr. McCosh never hesitates to bestow praise when merited nor to attack a heresy whenever found."—*Congregational Review.*

THE METHOD OF DIVINE GOVERNMENT.
Physical and Moral. 8vo, $2.00.

In this work Dr. McCosh shows that God is Governor as well as Preserver of His own works, and gives a searching view of Natural Law and Providence.

"It is refreshing to read a work so distinguished for originality and soundness of thinking, especially as coming from an author of our own country."
—*Sir William Hamilton.*

"Dr. McCosh's work is of the compact cast and thought-eliciting complexion which men do not willingly let die ; and we promise such of our readers as may possess themselves of it much entertainment and instruction of a high order, and a fund of solid thought, which they will not soon exhaust."—*Hugh Miller, in Witness.*

"This work is distinguished from other similar ones by its being based upon a thorough study of physical science, and an accurate knowledge of its present condition, and by its entering in a deeper and more unfettered manner than its predecessors upon the discussion of the appropriate psychological, ethical, and theological questions.—*Dr. Ulrici, in Zeitschrift für Philosophie.*

THE SCOTTISH PHILOSOPHY. Biograpical, Expository, Critical. From Hutcheson to Hamilton. 8vo, $2.00.

"This book contains a full exposition of the Scottish Philosophy. There is no other book on the subject. Dr. McCosh's expositions of philosophic doctrine are no less remarkable for their lucidity than their fairness. Nor is this volume confined to the mere analysis and exhibitions of speculative theories. It is enlivened with humorous personal details which present the great masters of Scotland in their domestic and social environment and make its perusal as attractive as it is informing. This elaborate work upon Scottish Philosophy cannot fail to be warmly welcomed by every student of speculative science."—*New Englander.*

THE NEW DEPARTURE IN COLLEGE EDUCATION. Net, 15 cents.

WHITHER? O, WHITHER? Net, 50 cents.

JUST PUBLISHED.

THE PREVAILING TYPES OF PHILOSOPHY. Can They Reach Reality Logically? Net, 75 cents.

In this work the author treats of the Experiential or Sensational; the *à priori* or Kantean; and the Scottish Schools which instead of assuming Reality try to prove it, and are driven by Herbert Spencer to Agnosticism. The aim of this work is to undermine Agnosticism and to shut us up into Realism.

☞ *Descriptive catalogue of distinguished works in all departments of education will be sent free on application. Examination terms allow instructors the privilege of returning specimens or purchasing them at examination price. Correspondence solicited.*

CHARLES SCRIBNER'S SONS, Publishers,

743 and 745 Broadway, New York.